Building Christian Discipline

EILEEN POLLINGER

BETHANY HOUSE PUBLISHERS
MINNEAPOLIS, MINNESOTA 55438
A Division of Bethany Fellowship, Inc.

Building Christian Discipline
Eileen Pollinger

ISBN 0–87123–877–2

Published by Bethany House Publishers
A Division of Bethany Fellowship, Inc.
6820 Auto Club Road, Minneapolis, Minnesota 55438

Printed in the United States of America

CONTENTS

INTRODUCTION

Building Christian Discipline is designed to give insights and guidelines on how to enter into the freedom and joy of living the way Jesus intended.

A discipline is an orderly or prescribed pattern of behavior. Christian disciplines are those patterns of behavior which conform to the example set by Christ.

The lessons in this book describe several disciplines and how to make them a part of one's life. They are not regimental rules to be followed exactly by every Christian. They are basic steps for learning to obey Christ's commandment: Love the Lord your God, and love your neighbor as yourself. Practicing them will work out a little differently for each individual, just like one's handwriting is a little different from anyone else's.

As we incorporate these disciplines into our lives, we discover they are not difficult or heavy, but instead relieve us of much of the load we carry. God commanded us to follow these disciplines as ways for Him to revive us, make us wise, and give us joy and light. As we live by them, we will find they are worth far more than gold and will lead us to God's rewards.

NOTE: The Challenge Activity at the end of most lessons is for those who would like to delve deeper. These assignments are not required as part of the lesson, but will be of benefit if you have time to do them.

LESSON 1

Getting Acquainted

1. What kind of person do you want to be five years from now?

2. What will it take to become that kind of person?

3. What does the word *discipline* mean to you?

4. What feelings does "discipline" arouse?

5. Look up "discipline" in a dictionary, then read the list of lesson headings in the Table of Contents. What relation do these have to your answer to question 3?

   How does this change your feelings about discipline?

6. Which disciplines in the Table of Contents do you practice regularly? (List by lesson number)
7. What effect do they have on your life?
8. Which have you never considered or tried?
9. What problems faced by most young adults might be resolved through learning discipline in these areas?

10. How many of these disciplines do you think you could make a part of your life during this course of study?

11. Which do you think are most important?
12. Which do you think are the most difficult to practice?
    Why?
13. Who do you know that tries to live by these disciplines?
14. What do you admire about that person?
15. What would you like to gain from this study?

SECTION 1

BASIC DISCIPLINES

As you may remember from last week's discussion, Christian discipline is a pattern of behavior which conforms to the example set by Christ. In order to become like Christ—God's goal for each of us—we must learn to do those things which transform us into His image.

The first nine disciplines we will study are basic, a necessary beginning for every Christian. They are the starting point from which the others progress. They stress a personal relationship with Christ, time spent in His presence. Ideally they are learned within the first few months of fellowship with Christ.

Yet it's never too late to start, for no Christian can keep right with God if he won't spend time with God daily. You can neglect almost anything else, but not Him.

Some of these disciplines you may be doing already, others may be new to you. As you learn each discipline, make an effort to incorporate it into your everyday life. Mastering these is essential to attaining the rest of the disciplines we will study.

LESSON 2

Fellowship Time

1. If you wanted to establish fellowship with someone, what would you do? ______________________________
2. Explain the purpose of daily fellowship with God. ______________________________
3. Fill in the chart on who met with God when:

Reference	*Person*	*Time of day*
Gen. 19:27	______________	______________
Ex. 34:2–4	______________	______________
1 Sam. 1:19	______________	______________
Job 1:5	______________	______________
Dan. 6:10	______________	______________
Mark 1:35	______________	______________

4. What part of the day is best for you to spend time with God? Why? ______________________________
5. Describe ideal conditions for a meeting place with God. ______________________________
6. Where is your best place in your present circumstances? ______________________________
7. What would you do during a time of fellowship with God? ______________________________
8. Estimate how long it would take. ______________________________
9. List things you would need. ______________________________
10. List the benefits of a written record of what you learn during your time with the Lord. ______________________________
11. What are possible positive results of fellowshiping with God? ______________________________
12. What do you do now to keep in daily fellowship with God? ______________________________
13. If you're now having a fellowship time, determine to meet with God daily. What might prevent you from carrying out this goal? ______________________________

CHALLENGE ACTIVITY: Survey several Christian leaders in your church or community to discover how they maintain daily fellowship time with God.

LESSON 3

Bible Reading

1. The importance of daily Bible reading:
   a. What will daily Bible reading do for me? (Ps. 19:7–11; Prov. 6:22; Jer. 15:16; John 5:24; 8:31, 32; Rom. 10:17; 15:4; 1 Pet. 2:2) ______
   b. What does the Bible call itself? (Dan. 10:21; Eph. 6:17; Col. 3:16; Heb. 6:5) ______
   c. What does the Bible say about itself? (Ps. 12:6; 19:7–11; Prov. 6:23; Isa. 55:11; Jer. 23:29; 2 Tim. 3:16, 17; Heb. 4:12) ______
   d. What importance does God put on the Bible? (Ps. 119:89; Isa. 40:8; Matt. 5:18; 24:35; Mark 13:31) ______
2. Underline which of these four methods of Bible reading you have used: (a) Read a Bible book; (b) Spend time rereading a single chapter; (c) Examine a Bible character; (d) Read on a specific topic.
3. The bottom line of Bible reading: *application!*

   Step 1: Determine what the Lord says concerning a problem or need in your life. Be open to hear what He wants you to know. Ask: What do You want me to learn about You? What teaching do I need to understand? What characteristic or quality is being taught? What warnings or commands are given?

   Exercise: Read 2 Kings 22:15–17. What did King Josiah learn about God and the people of Israel? ______

   Step 2: Examine your life in light of the biblical standard. Ask: What are my strengths? my weaknesses? Which area needs improvement most? Let the Holy Spirit examine you. He's far less critical than you are.

   Exercise: Read 2 Kings 22:11–13. How had the people not obeyed the commands? What needed to change? ______

   Step 3: Decide what you will do and how. Ask: What must I do to change my present attitudes and actions so they please God? How will I start? ______

   Exercise: What goal do you think King Josiah set for Israel? ______

   Step 4: Carry out your plan. Discuss your goals and steps with a fellow Christian who will encourage and pray for you.

   Exercise: Read 2 Kings 23:1–25. How did King Josiah get in step with God? ______
4. What application did you find for yourself in reading 2 Kings 22 and 23? ______
5. Getting started:
   a. How many minutes a day will I read the Bible this week? ______
   b. Which Bible reading method will I use? ______
   c. Which passage, chapter, or book will I choose? ______
   d. What do I hope to achieve from reading the Bible every day this week? ______

CHALLENGE ACTIVITY: Almost every verse of Ps. 119 refers to the Word of God. List as many verses as you can and state what they say the Word is, or does, or what you can do because of the Word.

FELLOWSHIP TIME ELEMENT: PRAYER

Prayer is an integral part of time spent with God. It is drawing near to God and talking to Him—just as you would talk to a person you love, trust, and respect. You share your feelings, hopes, disappointments, victories, and problems. In addition, you ask for—and take—what you need.

True prayer is recognizing our helplessness and God's adequacy—thus a statement of our faith in His willingness, even eagerness, to supply all our needs.

The next four lessons cover the elements that make up prayer.

LESSON 4

Prayer: Praise

1. If you were limited to only one thing you could praise God for, what would it be? ________________
2. Give three synonyms for praise. ________________
3. For what purpose were you created? (Isa. 43:21) ________________
4. Why should we praise God? (Ps. 9:11; Rev. 4:11) ________________
5. When are we to offer praise? (Ps. 35:28; 104:33; 145:1–2; Heb. 13:15) ________________
6. Read 1 Chron. 16:8–36. Record *reasons* and *ways* to praise God:

Reasons	*Ways*

7. Write a praise acrostic using your first and last names.
8. Read 1 Pet. 2:9. What are you doing now to fulfill the purpose of being a Christian stated there? ________________
9. What will you do this week to praise God? (Suggestions: Memorize a praise Psalm to say to God; record reasons to praise from your daily Bible reading, then praise Him; spend a fourth of your fellowship time praising God.)

CHALLENGE ACTIVITY: Make a praise notebook by recording praise verses which begin with each letter of the alphabet—a page for "a," a page for "b," etc.

LESSON 5

Prayer: Confession

1. Why is confessing sin necessary? (Ps. 66:18) ______
2. What do Ezra 10:11 and Jer. 3:13 say about confession of sin? ______
3. Using the references, match the sin with the confessing sinner:

Reference	*Sinner*	*Sin*
1 Sam. 15:24	____ Saul	1. Doubt
Luke 15:18	____ Prodigal Son	2. Coveting/Theft
Num. 22:34	____ Balaam	3. Waste, over-spending
Josh. 7:20	____ Achan	4. Greed
Luke 5:8	____ Peter	5. Adultery/Murder
2 Sam. 12:13	____ David	6. Disobedience

4. What does a person do when he confesses sin? ______
5. How important is confessing "small" sins, such as white lies, gossip, anger, making fun of someone, overeating, not making your bed, talking back to your parents? (Deut. 25:16; Ps. 5:4; Prov. 6:16–19; Zech. 8:17) ______
6. What things does God consider sin that non-Christians think are OK? Prov. 10:19, 14:21; Luke 16:13–15; John 3:36; 1 Cor. 6:9–10; James 4:17) ______
7. Look up Ps. 32:1–5 and 66:18; Prov. 28:13; 1 John 1:9. What results from lack of confession? ______

   from sincere confession? ______
8. How often do you think confession of sin is necessary? ______
9. Read Psalm 51.
   a. What did David ask for? (vv. 1, 2, 7, 9, 10) ______
   b. For what reasons did David expect forgiveness? (v. 1) ______
   c. What did David know God wanted of him? (vv. 6, 17) ______
   d. David had committed adultery and murder. Whom had he sinned against? (v. 4) ______
10. This week, ask God to reveal to you sins which need to be confessed. Following David's pattern in Psalm 51, "come clean" before God.

CHALLENGE ACTIVITY: Skim through the life of David to discover how he reacted when faced with his sins. The Old Testament gives two accounts of David's life. The first is found in 1 Sam. 16–31, 2 Sam. 1–24 and 1 Kings 1, 2. The second is found in 1 Chron. 10–29.

LESSON 6

Prayer: Thanksgiving

1. Consider why thanking God is essential to daily prayer life:
   a. Using a dictionary, define both praise and thanks. ______
   b. How do they differ? ______
   c. Check what the Bible commands regarding thanks: (1 Chron. 16:8; Ps. 100:4; Phil. 4:6; Col. 3:15) ______
2. When is the best time to give thanks to God?
   a. Ps. 119:62; 1 Chron. 23:30; Dan. 6:10 ______
   b. Ps. 30:12; Eph. 5:20; 1 Thess. 5:18 ______
3. Give thanks—for what?
   a. Discover what various people were grateful for:

Reference	*Who*	*What*
Ps. 7:17		
Ps. 75:1		
Ps. 118:29		
Dan. 2:23		
1 Cor. 15:57		
Col. 1:12		

   b. Read Phil. 1:12–19. Record four things Paul felt were worthy of thanks. ______
   c. What do these four items tell you about what to give thanks for? ______
4. How thankful are you?
   a. How long has it been since you thanked your mother for cooking meals for you? ______
   b. When did you last thank a friend for doing something nice? ______
   c. What would your grandparents say about your track record of sending thank-you notes for birthday and Christmas gifts? ______
5. How can you give thanks?
   a. Ps. 28:7 ______
   b. List three or four other ways to show thanks. ______
   c. Name five people who affect your life and what you could thank God for about each of them. Thank God. Write a thank-you note to one of them.
   d. Thank God for at least four things He has done in your life recently.

CHALLENGE ACTIVITY: Choose one situation in your life you'd do almost anything to get rid of or change. On a card, write the date and describe your circumstance and why you hate it. Make a commitment to thank God (for allowing it) every day for thirty days. At the end of that time, describe how you feel about the situation. What, if anything, has changed?

LESSON 7

Prayer: Intercession

1. God already knows what we need, so why do we pray? (1 Sam. 12:23; Prov. 15:8; Jer. 33:3; Luke 18:1; John 14:13; Phil. 4:6; 1 Tim. 2:1) ______

2. Intercessory prayer:
   a. Fill in the following chart:

Reference	*Person*	*Request*	*Reason*	*Answer*
Gen. 18:22–33				
Ex. 32:31–32				
Ex. 33:12–17				
1 Sam. 12:19, 23				
Job 42:10				

   b. What did Paul pray for in:
   Eph. 1:17–19 ______
   Phil. 1:9–11 ______
   Col. 1:9–14 ______
   1 Thess. 3:12–13 ______
   Philemon 6 ______
   c. According to Jer. 15:1, who were the "big" intercessors of the Old Testament? ______
   d. What attitudes are necessary in prayer? (2 Chron. 7:14; Jer. 29:13; Mark 11:24; James 5:16; 1 John 3:22) ______

3. Intercession for others:
   a. List the people who need your prayers. ______
   b. How can you pray for all of these within your available time? ______
   c. How can you remind yourself to pray for them? ______
   d. What would you pray for each? ______
   e. How will you know when God has answered a particular request? ______

4. Intercession for yourself:
   a. What are your needs today? ______
   b. How big does a need have to be before we take it to God? ______
   c. What would God think about your praying for good grades, your pet, a parking place, a boy/girl friend, or an item you don't need? ______

CHALLENGE ACTIVITY: Ask several people (including your Sunday School teacher, parents, brothers, sisters, pastor, or friends) to share a request about which you can pray. Pray daily, checking back to see what answers have been received.

LESSON 8

Memorization

1. How many verses have you memorized? ____0, ____1–30, ____31–100, ____over 100.
2. How many Bible chapters have you memorized? ____0, ____1–10, ____over 10.
3. If you have memorized Scripture, why did you do it? ____________________
4. If you haven't memorized Scripture, what has kept you from memorizing? ____________________
5. Check which benefits would motivate you to begin consistent memorizing:

____ Increased faith	____ Inner cleansing	____ Victory over sin
____ Guidance	____ Prayers answered	____ Knowing Bible doctrine
____ Bible study help	____ Finding verses	____ Holy Spirit awareness
____ Meditation	____ Aid to worship	____ Not wasting time
____ Counseling aid	____ Witnessing help	____ Teaching others
____ Overcoming bad habits	____ Transformed attitudes	____ Confidence

6. What does the Bible say about memorization? (Deut. 6:6, 11:18; Ps. 37:31; 119:11; Prov. 6:21; 7:3; 22:17–18) ____________________
7. List your prime reasons for memorizing Scripture. ____________________
8. Think of different ways to learn a verse. ____________________
9. What is your greatest difficulty in memorizing? ____________________
10. How would you choose what to memorize? ____________________
11. What memory project will you begin this week? ____________________

CHALLENGE ACTIVITY: Each person memorize the same passage in the same version and present it as a choral reading.

LESSON 9

Meditation

1. Many Eastern religions focus on meditation. How do you suppose meditation during a fellowship time with God differs from these? ____________________

2. What is the purpose of meditation? (Josh. 1:8; Ps. 19:14; 119:9, 11, 99) ____________________
3. When is a good time to meditate other than during your time with God? (Ps. 4:4; 63:6; 119:55, 148) ____________________

4. How does God want you to feel about meditating? (Ps. 1:2; 119:16, 97) ____________________

5. Read Rom. 12:1, 2.
   a. Read the two verses several times, emphasizing a different word or phrase each time. (Therefore, I *urge* you brothers, in view of . . . , then: Therefore, I urge you brothers, in *view of God's mercy* . . .) Read aloud if possible, listening to what the verse says with the different emphases.
   b. Put the verses in words you understand and are familiar with. ____________________

   c. Ask yourself the following questions:
      1) Who is the command directed to? ____________________
      2) What exactly is Paul telling you to do? ____________________
      3) Where can you carry out this command? ____________________
      4) When should you offer yourself to God? ____________________
      5) When should you strive for renewal in God? ____________________
      6) Why does God expect your dedication to Him? ____________________
      7) Why do you want to give yourself to God? ____________________
      8) How can you be a living sacrifice? ____________________
      9) How can you transform your mind? ____________________
   d. Read 2 Tim. 3:16, 17. What four functions does God's Word have? ____________________

      1) What truths has Rom. 12:1–2 taught you? ____________________

      2) What specific actions should you stop doing according to these verses? ____________________

      3) Is there something you should change to apply what you have learned? ________What? ____________________

      4) What would help you follow Rom. 12:1–2? ____________________

6. In responding to question 5, you have been meditating on Rom. 12:1–2. During the coming week, follow the same process, asking similar questions about Eph. 4:20–24. Record your findings in your fellowship time notebook.

CHALLENGE ACTIVITY: Meditate on the verse you memorized last week whenever you have a free moment: waiting for a class to begin, on your way to or from school, when you can't sleep.

LESSON 10

Bible Study

1. Complete the following steps to learn one way to study the Bible:
   a. Pray that you will be open to what God has to reveal in the passage.
   b. Read Gen. 12:1–9 five times (in different versions if possible).
   c. In column "b," rewrite each verse in your own words. Look up unfamiliar words, cross-references, and find places on a map to understand the content.
   d. In column "a," write a brief synopsis of the verse—as short as possible, while still giving you a handle to remember what the verse says. You may want to combine two or three verses in one synopsis.
   e. Divide the passage into three or four major sections at logical points. Mark these sections with dashes in the border between columns "b" and "c."
   f. Write a name for each section in column "c." If you can make each name start with the same letter, the sections are easier to remember.

   Column a | Column b | Column c

   g. Write an application you think God would have you put into your life for each section. ______
   h. Summarize the main teaching of the passage in a complete sentence of ten words or less. ______
2. What is the main difference between Bible *study* and Bible *reading* as outlined for a daily fellowship time? ______
3. How often do you think you should study the Bible? ______
4. What benefits are there in studying? ______

CHALLENGE ACTIVITY: Choose a passage that interests you and study it this week using the steps you have learned.

SECTION 2

GROWTH DISCIPLINES

As Christians we're not to become stagnant, but to be continually growing in all those things which make us more like Jesus. God commands in 2 Pet. 3:18 to grow. In Phil. 1:6, He promises us growth, and He tells us in 1 John 3:2 that growth is a lifelong process for Christians.

This section of disciplines contains those which God designed to help His children grow beyond the basics into maturity. These disciplines are not always popular or pleasant to learn and practice, but reap great rewards both in this life and in the life to come.

LESSON 11

Teachability

1. What is your usual response when someone corrects you? ______

2. What teachable responses do you find in Prov. 10:17; 15:31; 24:32? ______

3. What attitude does David warn against in Ps. 32:8, 9? ______
4. What attitude does Solomon prescribe in Prov. 11:2? ______
5. What attitude does Paul describe in Phil. 3:12–16? ______
6. What consequences followed unteachable attitudes?

	Attitude	*Consequence*
a. 2 Chron. 16:7–12		
b. 2 Chron. 25:14–16		
c. 2 Chron. 26:16–20		
d. Prov. 10:8		
e. Prov. 13:13, 18		

7. Which consequences may apply to people today? ______
8. What two things happened when Naaman became teachable and obedient? (2 Kings 5:9–18) ______

9. Who did David learn from in 1 Sam. 25:32–33? ______
10. Who can you learn from if you have a teachable heart? ______
11. What three "teachers" are found in Prov. 6:23? ______
12. Why does God want us to be teachable? (Heb. 12:5–6) ______

13. What are God's purposes? (Heb. 12:10–11) ______
14. Rate your teachable attitudes on a scale from 1 to 10. ______
15. What attitude will you work at changing this week to become more teachable? ______

16. How will you go about it? ______

CHALLENGE ACTIVITY: Study Prov. 1:20–33 to find attitudes which lead to teachability, or non-teachability and the results of each. What attitudes do you need to develop?

LESSON 12

Waiting

1. Name one thing you can't have now but must wait for. _____
2. How do you feel about waiting? _____
3. How does God want you to feel? (Ps. 27:14; 37:7; Mic. 7:7) _____
4. Check the definitions you think refer to waiting:
   1. _____ Looking forward expectantly
   2. _____ Holding back expectantly
   3. _____ Being ready and available
5. Read Ex. 2:1–7.
   a. Which of the above definitions do you think would describe the way Miriam waited as she watched the basket that held her brother? _____
   b. Which would describe her waiting (without dashing to the rescue) as she watched Pharaoh's daughter find Moses? _____
   c. Which describes her proposition to Pharaoh's daughter? _____
6. Scan Gen. 25:19–26 and 27:1–17. Which, if any, of the three kinds of waiting did Rebekah exhibit? _____
7. List some things to wait for, looking forward expectantly. (Ps. 5:3; Titus 2:13; James 1:5; 1 John 3:2) _____
8. What goes on in our lives during this waiting time? (Phil. 1:6; 2 Tim. 2:15) _____
9. In holding back expectantly, do you think you would _____ sit back and do nothing? _____ help God by figuring out the best solution? _____ assume God will do what's necessary at the right time?
10. What is needed to wait, holding back expectantly? (Isa. 8:17) _____
11. Read Eph. 2:10 to find why we need to be ready and available. _____
12. What do we have to do to be ready? (Luke 11:1; Rom. 12:6–8; 1 Pet. 2:2) _____
13. What is being available? (Ps. 143:10; Eph. 6:6) _____
14. Record rewards for waiting. (Isa. 30:18; Isa. 64:4) _____
15. How are you at waiting? _____
16. What will you do this week to grow in the discipline of waiting? _____

CHALLENGE ACTIVITY: Keep track of your attitudes and reactions to waiting—a column for expectant waiting, one for non-waiting or grumbling. If you've more points for waiting, reward yourself with a special treat. If you've been a non-waiter, cut out an hour of TV or a favorite dessert.

LESSON 13

Perseverance/Patience

1. How many projects have you started in the last three months? __________
2. How many are finished? ______ In progress? ______ Left unfinished? ______
3. Which of the disciplines studied so far are now a part of your everyday life? __________
4. What is your toughest subject in school? __________
5. Do you stick with the assignments until you understand? __________
6. What irritates you the most frequently? __________
7. How do you react to irritations? __________
8. How do you respond when someone tries to convince you a false teaching is right? __________
9. How would you rate yourself on patience/perseverance? 1 2 3 4 5
10. What is God's instruction regarding patience and perseverance? (1 Cor. 15:58; Gal. 5:1; Heb. 12:1; James 5:7; 1 Pet. 5:9) __________
11. List the end results. (Gal. 6:9; Heb. 10:36; James 1:4, 12) __________
12. Analyze 1 Kings 13:1–24 for insights on perseverance. __________
13. Name one area in which you need to practice patience/perseverance this week. ______ Write down two specific things you can do to help yourself be patient and persevere when you meet something difficult this week. __________

CHALLENGE ACTIVITY: Read Dan. 3:1–30. Imagine what the characters mentioned must have felt. Try to determine how you would react under the same conditions. Record insights which might help you persevere in your Christian walk.

LESSON 14

Suffering

1. Why do you think a loving, kind God allows suffering? (2 Cor. 1:3–4; Heb. 12:4–11) ______
2. What reason does Jesus give for suffering? (John 15:18–21) ______
3. Explain what suffering is. ______
4. All Christians suffer ______. (1 Cor. 10:13; James 1:13)
5. What attitude does the Bible teach regarding suffering? (Hab. 3:17–18; Acts 5:41; Rom. 5:3; 1 Pet. 4:12–13) ______
6. What do we rejoice about when we suffer? ______
7. List promised outcomes for enduring suffering. (Ps. 34:19; Isa. 43:2; 2 Cor. 4:17) ______
8. What are purposes of suffering? (Ps. 66:10; Isa. 48:10; 1 Pet. 1:7) ______
9. From your observation, which of these reactions to suffering is most normal? ____ Grin and bear it, ____ Pray to get rid of it, ____ Figure a way to beat it, ____ Work to discover the benefits, ____ Get depressed.
10. How does God expect us to go through suffering? (2 Cor. 4:1, 16; Eph. 3:13) ______
11. List the rewards promised to those in the seven churches who overcome affliction and suffering. Check the one(s) which most appeal to you:
    Rev. 2:7—Ephesus ______
    Rev. 2:11—Smyrna ______
    Rev. 2:17—Pergamum ______
    Rev. 2:26–28—Thyatira ______
    Rev. 3:5—Sardis ______
    Rev. 3:12—Philadelphia ______
    Rev. 3:21—Laodicea ______
12. What suffering would be most difficult for you to endure? ______ Why? ______
13. How can what you've learned in this lesson affect your life this week? ______

CHALLENGE ACTIVITY: Psalm 119 provides insights about the right response to suffering. Record your thoughts on verses 50, 67, 71, 75, 86, 87, 92, 107, 143, 153, and 161.

SECTION 3

LIFESTYLE DISCIPLINES

The next ten lessons deal with disciplines which eventually become a normal part of the Christian's lifestyle. That is, they will if the individual discovers what they are and works to apply them to everyday situations.

The ultimate goal of each of these disciplines is to please God by the way we live. You may already be a long way down the road with some of them—some may need some work, others may be new to you. Work through them with a heart open to become the person God designed you to be and enjoy the blessings God promises as you do.

LESSON 15

Commitment

1. How do you feel when someone breaks a promise or cancels a date? ______
2. How often do you agree to a plan and then change your mind? ______
3. To what degree should we keep commitments? (Ps. 15:4) ______
4. List some commitments that might be better for a Christian teen to break. ______
5. What might keep you from making or keeping a commitment to give your life to God? (Personal) ______

   Prov. 6:6–11 ______ 1 Pet. 4:3–4 ______
   Prov. 13:20 ______ 1 John 4:18 ______
   Col. 3:5 ______ Rev. 3:15–16 ______
6. Define spiritual commitment using Josh. 23:8, Luke 9:62, and Phil. 1:27. ______
7. Look up the following verses to find what God wants us to commit to:

   Deut. 6:5 ______ Rom. 12:11 ______
   Ps. 119:2 ______ Gal. 6:9 ______
   Prov. 3:5 ______ Titus 3:1 ______
8. Match the men with the commitments they made:

Josh. 14:8	1—Caleb	____ Worshiped God only
1 Kings 13:8	2—A man of God	____ Headed for certain death
2 Kings 22:2	3—Josiah	____ Did right in God's eyes
Job 23:11	4—Job	____ Chose to obey God rather than eat
Dan. 3:18	5—Shadrach	____ Finished his task
Luke 9:51	6—Jesus	____ Kept God's way
Acts 4:19–20	7—Peter & John	____ Followed God wholeheartedly
Acts 20:24	8—Paul	____ Obeyed God rather than men

9. What is awarded to those who keep commitments to God?

   Matt. 10:32 ______ Heb. 12:7 ______
10. What commitments has God made to you?

    Mark 11:24 ______ Acts 10:35 ______
    John 5:24 ______ 2 Pet. 1:3–4 ______
11. Does God always keep His commitments? ______
12. What commitments have you made to God? ______
13. How well have you kept them? ______
14. Read the commitment choices in question 7. What will you choose to commit to this week? ______

CHALLENGE ACTIVITY: Using the Bible study method you learned in Lesson 10, study Deut. 30:11–20 to discover more insights about commitment.

LESSON 16

Diligence

1. What encouragements to be diligent does the Bible offer us?

Prov. 10:4 ____________________ 1 Cor. 15:58 ____________________

Prov. 12:24 ____________________ Heb. 11:6 ____________________

Prov. 13:4 ____________________ 2 Pet. 1:10–11 ____________________

2. Mark the following statements true or false:

____ Diligence in things like neatness and courtesy is as important as diligence in Bible reading and honesty. (1 Cor. 10:31)

____ Spiritual maturity is gained by diligent effort. (Heb. 5:14)

____ Diligence is the key ingredient in pleasing God. (Heb. 11:6)

____ Laziness keeps a person from being diligent. (2 Thess. 3:11)

____ Diligence is application of truths we've learned. (Luke 6:47)

3. In what areas does God urge us to be diligent?

Deut. 6:17 ____________________ Phil. 3:13–14 ____________________

1 Chron. 22:19 ____________________ 2 Tim. 4:2 ____________________

Prov. 4:23 ____________________ Heb. 6:10–12 ____________________

Eccles. 9:10 ____________________ 2 Pet. 1:5 ____________________

John 9:4 ____________________ 2 Pet. 3:14 ____________________

4. In which of these are you most diligent? ____________________

5. In which one are you least diligent? ____________________

6. What will you do this week to become more diligent in this area? ____________________

____

CHALLENGE ACTIVITY: Read 1 Tim. 4:15, then determine exactly what Timothy is to do to make such a difference in his life that others would see the change.

LESSON 17

Godliness/Holiness

1. Why do we need to become holy? (Isa. 64:6–7) ______
2. Why should we become holy?
   2 Cor. 7:1 ______
   1 Thess. 4:7 ______
   2 Tim. 2:21 ______
   Heb. 12:14 ______
   1 Pet. 1:16 ______
   2 Pet. 3:11 ______
3. List three ingredients that make up an attitude of holiness:
   ______ Isa. 66:2; 2 Cor. 7:1
   ______ 1 John 4:9–10; 2 Cor. 5:14–15
   ______ Ps. 42:1–2 and 63:1; Phil. 3:10
4. List the marks of a holy or godly Christian. (Ps. 15:1–5; Rom. 12:9–21; James 2:14–26) ______
5. How can we become holy?
   Rom. 5:19 ______
   1 Thess. 3:13 ______
   Titus 2:11–12 ______
   Heb. 12:10 ______
   2 Pet. 1:3 ______
6. How do we stay holy?
   Prov. 16:17 ______
   Isa. 35:8 ______
   Rom. 12:2 ______
   Rom. 13:14 ______
   1 Cor. 6:18–19 ______
   Gal. 5:16 ______
   Col. 3:1–2 ______
   Heb. 12:1 ______
   James 4:7 ______
   2 Pet. 3:14 ______
7. After studying about holiness and godliness, how would you rate yourself? ______ 1, ______ 2, ______ 3, ______ 4, ______ 5, ______ 6, ______ 7, ______ 8, ______ 9, ______ 10
8. Choose one area in which you want to increase your "holiness quotient" and decide what you can do this week to pursue godliness. ______

CHALLENGE ACTIVITY: Study these verses for insights on how to live a godly and holy life in the midst of ungodliness: 1 Cor. 5:9–10; Eph. 5:5–12; Phil. 2:14–15; 2 Pet. 2:7–9.

OR

Study the book of Jude, looking for descriptions of both godliness and ungodliness. You will find 25 ungodly characteristics and 17 godly.

LESSON 18

Humility/Meekness

1. What is your opinion of humility? ______________________
   of meekness? ______________________
2. Which definitions fit your idea of humility and meekness?
   ____ Enduring injury with patience and without resentment
   ____ Deficient in spirit and courage
   ____ Not violent or strong
   ____ Spirit of deference/submission
   ____ Ranking low in hierarchy
   ____ Power under control
   ____ Freedom from pride
3. What is God's opinion of humility?
   Prov. 22:4 ______________________
   Prov. 29:23 ______________________
   Isa. 57:15 ______________________
   Matt. 18:4 ______________________
4. Who was the meekest man? (Num. 12:3) __________ What was his standing with God? (Ex. 33:17) ____
   ____
5. Examine God's commands regarding humility and meekness.
   Mic. 6:8 ______________________
   Luke 22:26 ______________________
   Eph. 4:2 ______________________
   James 4:10 ______________________
6. What effect would obedience to these have on your life? ______________________
   ____
7. What attitudes/actions show humility and meekness?
   Prov. 27:2 ______________________
   Matt. 20:26 ______________________
   Luke 14:10 ______________________
   1 Pet. 5:5–6 ______________________
8. Which of these can you put into practice this week? ______________________
   What will you do? ______________________

CHALLENGE ACTIVITY: Search Isa. 50:5–6; Zech. 9:9; Matt. 9:10, 21:5, 27:12–14; John 8:50, 13:5; Acts 8:32–33; 2 Cor. 8:9; Phil. 2:8–9; and 1 Pet. 2:23 to discover Christ's example of humility and meekness.

LESSON 19

Self-control

1. Which of the following do you have trouble controlling?

_____ Anger _____ Envy _____ Bitterness
_____ Lust _____ Thoughts _____ Appetite
_____ Selfishness _____ Tongue _____ Pride

2. What is the Bible view of self-control?

Prov. 25:28 ____________________ Titus 2:11–12 ____________________
1 Thess. 5:6–8 ____________________ 1 Pet. 4:7 ____________________

3. Complete the following chart. Under each reference, write what the Bible says about that item.

Problem	Description	Command	Consequence	Prescription
Anger		Ps. 37:8 Eccles. 7:9 Eph. 4:31	Prov. 14:17 Matt 5:22	Prov. 16:32
Lust		Prov. 6:25 Rom. 6:12 Col. 3:5 1 Pet. 2:11	James 1:15	Gal. 5:16 2 Tim. 2:22
Selfishness	Matt. 25:43	Rom. 14:21		1 Cor. 10:24 Phil. 2:4

Envy		Ps. 37:1 Gal. 5:26 1 Pet. 2:1	Prov. 14:30	Prov. 23:17 1 Cor. 13:4
Thoughts	Prov. 15:26 Rom. 8:7	Eph. 4:17	Prov. 24:9 Rom. 1:21	Jer. 4:14
Tongue	Rom. 3:13–14	Ps. 34:13 Eccles. 5:2	Matt. 12:36–37 James 1:26	Prov. 21:23 1 Pet. 3:10
Bitterness		Eph. 4:31	Heb. 12:15	
Appetite	Eccles. 6:7 Isa. 56:11–12		Prov. 23:20–21 Luke 21:34 Phil. 3:19	Prov. 23:1–2
Pride	Prov. 21:4 1 Cor. 8:2 James 4:16	Prov. 25:6–7 Rom. 12:16	Prov. 16:18 James 4:6	James 4:10

4. In which area is God prodding you to make changes? ______________________________

5. What can you do this week to be more self-controlled? ______________________________

____

CHALLENGE ACTIVITY: The Bible says the tongue is the most difficult to control. Study James 3:1–12 to discover all you can about this problem in self-control.

LESSON 20

Fellowship

1. Read Heb. 10:25. What does this verse tell us to do and why? ______

2. Who set examples of attending services?
   Luke 4:16 ______ Acts 13:13–14 ______
3. What are two good reasons for going to church?
   Ps. 84:4 ______ Mic. 4:2 ______
4. Whom does God want us to have fellowship with?
   Mal. 3:16 ______ 1 John 1:3 ______
   1 Cor. 1:9 ______ Rev. 3:20 ______
5. What are evidences of friendship or fellowship?
   Prov. 17:17 ______ Prov. 27:17 ______
   Prov. 27:10 ______ John 15:13–14 ______
6. Note some benefits of fellowship:
   Eccles. 4:9–10 ______ Matt. 18:19–20 ______
7. List the commands concerning how we should relate to other Christians:
   1 Cor. 1:10 ______
   Phil. 1:27 ______
   Phil. 2:3–4 ______
   1 Pet. 3:8 ______
8. How is this unity possible?
   Rom. 12:5 ______ Eph. 4:13 ______
9. Other than church, what opportunities are available for fellowship? ______

10. To what extent should a Christian teen fellowship with non-Christians? ______
    Why? ______
    Cite biblical examples. ______
11. What can you do to fellowship in unity with others this week? ______

CHALLENGE ACTIVITY: Read Nehemiah 4. List all evidences you can find of the unity of believers being the key to completing their task. What can you learn from this incident to change your attitudes or actions?

LESSON 21

Stewardship

1. What is stewardship? ______
2. What additional information do you find in 1 Cor. 4:1–2 and 1 Tim. 6:20? ______
3. Explain the difference between a steward and an owner. ______
4. Who is the owner for whom we act as stewards? (Ps. 24:1) ______
5. What is His claim on us? (Deut. 32:6; Mark 10:45) ______

   ______
6. To what degree does our owner hold us accountable?

   Matt. 12:36 ______

   Luke 12:48 ______

   Rom. 14:12 ______

   1 Pet. 4:5 ______
7. In each of the following categories, jot down what you think good stewardship would be and then what your performance is:

	Good stewardship	*Your performance*
Time	______	______
Speech	______	______
Health (Body)	______	______
Money/Possessions	______	______
Spiritual Gifts	______	______

8. In which of the above categories do you need to improve most? ______
9. What will you do this week to begin becoming a better steward? ______

   ______

CHALLENGE ACTIVITY: Read Matt. 25:14–30. Discover why each steward was given what he was given, what he did with it, and the results. From this parable, what can you learn about being a good steward?

LESSON 22

Submission

1. Mark the following statements true or false:
   - a. _____ Submission is an important part of the way God wants me to live.
   - b. _____ My spiritual peace depends to a great extent on how well I submit.
   - c. _____ Since I have freedom in Christ, I needn't submit to anyone but God.
   - d. _____ I'm expected to submit to everyone.
   - e. _____ I submit to others mainly for Christ's sake.
   - f. _____ If someone in authority isn't kind to me, I don't have to submit.
   - g. _____ Submission is as important now as it was in Bible times.
   - h. _____ I have the final authority over my life.
   - i. _____ The limits of my parents' authority changes with time.
   - j. _____ I need submit only to people I want to submit to.
   - k. _____ Submission means surrender.
   - l. _____ The final and total authority in my life is God.
   - m. _____ I serve God when I submit to the people He has given authority over me.
2. Who is our authority? (Matt. 28:18) ____________________
3. What does God ask for? (Prov. 23:26; Rom. 12:1) ____________________
4. Whom do we need to submit to?
   Eph. 6:1 ____________________ James 4:7 ____________________
   Eph. 6:5–9 ____________________ 1 Pet. 2:13–14 ____________________
   Heb. 13:17 ____________________
5. To whom should we refuse to submit? (Acts 4:18–20; 1 Pet. 5:8–9) ____________________
   ____
6. Explore the attitudes necessary for godly submission:
   Ps. 40:8 ____________________ Eph. 6:6 ____________________
   Eph. 5:21 ____________________ 1 Pet. 2:17 ____________________
7. List a couple of the results of being submissive:
   Matt. 12:50 ____________________
   John 7:17 ____________________
8. To whom do you have the most trouble submitting? ____________________
9. Why? ____________________
10. What would God have you do about it? ____________________

CHALLENGE ACTIVITY: Talk to a parent (other than your own), a policeman, and a teacher. Ask what they think about teens who submit to authorities willingly versus those who rebel and go their own way. Find out what they have seen resulting from teens' submission or rebellion.

LESSON 23

Obedience

1. Why is obedience difficult? ______
2. What two factors make it easier? John 14:15, 31 ______
   Deut. 9:23 ______
3. Check the penalties for disobedience:
   1 Sam. 12:15 ______ 2 Thess. 1:8 ______
   Eph. 5:6 ______ Heb. 3:18 ______
4. What does God command? To what degree or expectation?
   Deut. 26:16 ______ ______
   Josh. 1:8 ______ ______
   Matt. 7:21 ______ ______
   1 John 3:23 ______ ______
5. What does Jesus say to obey? What is the result?
   Matt. 7:24 ______ ______
   Matt. 12:50 ______ ______
   John 14:23 ______ ______
6. Study these biblical examples of obedience:

Reference	*Who*	*What he did*	*How much, how well, or how quickly*
Gen. 6:22			
Josh. 11:15			
2 Kings 18:6			
Matt. 4:18–20			
Luke 2:22, 39			
Acts 26:19			
Your name:			

7. As Jesus looks at your obedience, would He discipline or could He give what He promises in 1 John 3:22?
   ______
8. What command will you obey this week that has been a problem before? ______
   ______

CHALLENGE ACTIVITY: Turn to Genesis 22. Record in your notebook all the facts about this story of Abraham's obedience. Also, put yourself in Isaac's place. He was a young man your age or a little older. What must he have felt? Why didn't he resist? What would you have done?

LESSON 24

Fruit-bearing

1. Why did God choose you to be a Christian? (John 15:16; Rom. 7:4)

2. Name character traits included in fruitfulness. (Isa. 32:17; Gal. 5:22–23; Eph. 5:9)

3. Define any of these you are unsure of.

4. How do we gain the character traits of fruitfulness?

   Matt. 12:35

   John 15:2

   John 15:4–5

   Rom. 6:22

   2 Cor. 9:10

   Gal. 5:22

   Phil. 1:11

   Heb. 6:9

   Heb. 12:11

   James 3:18

5. What is the purpose of being fruitful?

   John 15:8 Phil. 1:11

6. Which of the character traits that make up fruitfulness are lacking or weak in your life?

7. Which one will you start developing this week?

   How?

CHALLENGE ACTIVITY: Read Matt. 5:20–48. Log in your notebook the level of righteousness Christ expects of His people in each of the areas covered.

SECTION 4

GODWARD DISCIPLINES

This section deals with those disciplines which enhance and build our intimate relationship with God. Through these disciplines, we begin to know Him, to appreciate His greatness and glory, and to respond to Him as He wants us to—in humility and love. More than any others, these four disciplines can draw us close to the Lord.

LESSON 25

Reverence

1. What is your opinion of God? _____
2. What does the Bible call reverence? (Ps. 33:8) _____
3. What does "fear the Lord" mean to you? _____
4. What does the Bible say fearing the Lord is?

   Job 28:28 _____ Prov. 8:13 _____
5. What does the Bible tell us about fearing the Lord?

   Josh. 24:14 _____

   1 Sam. 12:24 _____

   Ps. 36:1 _____

   Ps. 147:11 _____

   Prov. 16:6 _____

   Eccles. 12:13 _____
6. What reasons does the Bible give for holding God in reverence?

   Ps. 33:8–11 _____ 1 Pet. 1:17 _____

   Ps. 89:7 _____ Rev. 15:4 _____
7. What effect does fearing the Lord have in our lives?

   Ex. 20:20 _____

   Ps. 103:11 _____

   Ps. 145:19 _____

   Ps. 147:11 _____

   Isa. 33:6 _____

   2 Cor. 5:11, 20 _____
8. How do we fear the Lord?

   Deut. 6:2 _____

   Deut. 31:11–12 _____

   Ps. 34:11–14 _____

   Ps. 86:11 _____

   Prov. 2:1–5 _____
9. To what extent do you fear the Lord? _____
10. What aspect of God's character do you reverence most? _____
11. How can you show more reverence for God this week? _____

CHALLENGE ACTIVITY: Skim through Proverbs, underlining in yellow pencil every mention of fear of the Lord. Go back and read the underlined verses, recording any insights in your notebook.

LESSON 26

Worship

1. When was the last time you worshiped God? ____
2. What do you do when you worship? ____
3. We are to worship God because of:

   Who He is:

   Ex. 15:11 ____

   Job 37:22–23 ____

   Ps. 89:5–8 ____

   Isa. 28:29 ____

   Isa. 46:5, 9 ____

   What He does:

   Neh. 9:6 ____

   Jer. 32:27 ____

   Rom. 4:21 ____

   2 Cor. 9:8 ____

   Eph. 3:20 ____

   Heb. 7:25 ____

   What He possesses:

   1 Chron. 29:11–12 ____

   Ps. 24:1 ____

   Ps. 50:10–12 ____

   Ps. 95:3–5 ____
4. What do you learn about worship in:

   Ex. 20:3 ____

   Ps. 29:2 ____

   Ps. 95:6 ____

   Ps. 99:9 ____

   Ps. 100:2 ____

   Matt. 4:10 ____

   Mark 12:30 ____

   Rom. 12:1 ____
5. Find the attitudes for worship in:

   Ps. 5:7 ____

   Eccles. 5:1 ____

   Hab. 2:20 ____

   John 4:23–24 ____
6. How will you put into practice what you have learned about worshiping God? ____

CHALLENGE ACTIVITY: Copy Prov. 3:5–6 on a card and carry it with you through the week in a way you will see it often. Each time you read the verse, remind yourself to *acknowledge* Him (know actively the presence of God). Be as conscious as you can that every moment, whatever you're doing, the magnificent, holy, powerful God is with you. Record your feelings and any new insights about worship in your notebook.

LESSON 27

Faith

1. What evidence have you experienced that God is worthy of your faith? ____________________
____

2. Complete the chart on the experiences of these Bible characters:

Reference	*Who*	*What expected*	*Result*
1 Sam. 17:37, 49–50	______	______	______
2 Chron. 20:12–22	______	______	______
Dan. 3:17–27	______	______	______
Matt. 8:2–3	______	______	______
Matt. 15:21–28	______	______	______
Acts 27:22–44	______	______	______

3. What is faith? (Heb. 11:1) ____________________

4. How important is having faith in God?
   Rom. 14:23 ____________________ Gal. 5:6 ____________________
   2 Cor. 5:7 ____________________ Heb. 11:6 ____________________

5. How do we get faith?
   John 20:31 ____________________ Rom. 10:17 ____________________

6. How can we increase our faith?
   Mark 9:24 ____________________ Rom. 4:18–21 ____________________

7. How do we demonstrate that we have faith?
   James 2:14–17 ____________________ 1 John 5:4 ____________________

8. Whom or what we have faith in is as important as having faith. Match the following needs with whom or what you are *now* depending on to meet them: (a) eternal life; (b) your next meal; (c) choice of the right career; (d) choice of a spouse; (e) meeting your everyday needs; (f) decisions about college; (g) decisions on what activities to participate in; (h) victory over sin.

   _____ Myself _____ Friends _____ School counselors
   _____ Parents _____ Chance _____ Money
   _____ Personality _____ God _____ Living a good life

9. What would you be willing to do this week to increase your faith in God? ____________________
____

CHALLENGE ACTIVITY: Choose an older person who you feel demonstrates living by faith and interview him/her. Ask how he learned about faith, what events in his life increased his faith, what he would recommend to a young Christian regarding building faith. Record your findings in your notebook and consider following them.

LESSON 28

Fasting

1. What is the longest total fast on record? (Ex. 34:28) ______
   Who fasted? ______ What was he doing? ______
2. How long can a person live without food? ______ Without water? ______
3. What did people do along with fasting?
   Neh. 1:4 ______
   Ps. 35:13 ______
   Joel 2:12 ______
   Acts 13:2–3 ______
4. For what purpose did people fast?
   Neh. 1:3–4 ______
   Esther 4:16 ______
   Acts 13:3 ______
   Acts 14:23 ______
5. What does God tell us about fasting?
   Isa. 58:3–7 ______
   Zech. 7:5 ______
   Matt. 6:16–18 ______
6. What was the only fast commanded, its purpose, and frequency? (Lev. 16:29–31) ______
   ______
7. What do these New Testament references reveal about fasting today?
   Matt. 6:16–18 ______
   Mark 2:18–20 ______
8. What do you believe about fasting in our time? ______
9. What do you need to do to practice what you believe? ______

CHALLENGE ACTIVITY: If you have no health problems such as diabetes, heart trouble, hypoglycemia, try a partial fast—from lunch to lunch or dinner to dinner, missing two meals. In order to do more than just deny yourself food, spend the 24 hours focusing on God, meditating on Scripture, and praying. This can be done while you're continuing normal activities. Record what you feel and learn in your notebook.

SECTION 5

MANWARD DISCIPLINES

The last six disciplines we will study are those which take us into the realm of serving others. Jesus' ministry was aimed at winning men to himself and making them like Him, and we are now at the point where we begin to focus our growth in that direction.

As you complete these lessons, begin to look around you and become aware of the needs, hurts, wants of people. What can you do to help? What service can you give that will draw them closer to Jesus?

LESSON 29

Love

1. Why is love important in our lives? ______
2. Whom are we to love? ______
   Matt. 5:44 ______ John 15:17 ______
   Luke 10:27 ______ 1 Pet. 2:17 ______
3. How are we to love?
   John 13:34 ______ 1 Pet. 1:22 ______
   Heb. 13:1 ______ John 15:13 ______
4. What are some purposes of loving?
   Prov. 10:12 ______ Heb. 10:24 ______
   Rom. 13:8 ______ 1 Pet. 4:8 ______
5. How is love described?
   Rom. 12:9 ______ 2 John 6 ______
   1 Cor. 13:4–7 ______
   ______
6. How can we show love?
   Matt. 18:21–22 ______ Eph. 4:2 ______
   Luke 3:10–14 ______ 1 John 3:17–18 ______
7. How is it possible for us to love?
   Phil. 1:9 ______ 1 Thess. 4:9 ______
   Col. 1:4–5 ______ 1 Tim. 1:5 ______
8. Examples of love in action:

Reference	*Who*	*For whom*	*What*
Rom. 16:4	______	______	______
2 Cor. 12:15	______	______	______
2 Tim. 1:16–17	______	______	______
Your experience	______	______	______

9. How would your friends and family rate your love in action? ______
10. What will you do this week to demonstrate God's love in your life? ______
    ______

CHALLENGE ACTIVITY: Study 1 John 4:7–21, using the method you learned in Lesson 10.

LESSON 30

Giving

1. Why do you think God asks us to give? ______
2. What should we give?
   Matt. 25:35–40 ______ Heb. 6:10 ______
   Eph. 4:28 ______ Heb. 13:16 ______
3. How much should we give?
   Deut. 16:17 ______
   Acts 11:29 ______
   2 Cor. 8:3, 12 ______
4. Where do we get what we give?
   Deut. 8:18 ______
   1 Chron. 29:12 ______
5. What reasons do you find for giving?
   Ex. 25:2 ______
   Prov. 3:9 ______
   2 Cor. 8:7 ______
   1 Tim. 6:18–19 ______
6. How shall we give?
   Matt. 6:1, 3 ______ 1 Cor. 16:2 ______
   Rom. 12:8 ______ 2 Cor. 9:7 ______
7. Whom do we give to?
   Deut. 15:7 ______
   Rom. 12:13 ______
   1 Cor. 9:14 ______
   Heb. 13:2–3 ______
8. Notice some results of giving/non-giving:

   Giving:
   Prov. 11:24 ______
   Prov. 28:27 ______
   2 Cor. 9:12 ______

   Non-giving:
   Prov. 21:13 ______
   Mal. 3:8 ______
9. What have you given within the past month? ______
10. What will you do this week to comply with this discipline? ______

CHALLENGE ACTIVITY: Meditate (see Lesson 9) on 2 Cor. 8:1–15 during the coming week to gain wisdom on giving.

LESSON 31

Service

1. What images come to mind when you hear the word service or serving? ____________________

____

2. What effect do they have on your desire to serve? ____________________
3. What are God's expectations of us in relation to service?

Deut. 10:12 ____________________

Mark 1:18 ____________________

Mark 10:43–44 ____________________

John 12:26 ____________________

4. Whom should we serve?

Matt. 4:10 ____________________ Gal. 6:10 ____________________

5. What kinds of things do we do?

Eccles. 9:10 ____________________

Matt. 25:35 ____________________

Luke 10:37 ____________________

2 Cor. 1:4 ____________________

Gal. 6:2, 10 ____________________

Heb. 10:24 ____________________

6. What sources of strength do we have for serving?

Acts 1:8 ____________________ Eph. 4:11–12 ____________________

Rom. 12:6–8 ____________________ 2 Tim. 2:21 ____________________

7. What can you learn from these examples of service?

Reference	*Who*	*What*	*How well*
Gen. 6:22			
2 Chron. 24:5			
2 Chron. 25:2			
Isa. 6:8			
Luke 10:30–36			
John 4:34			

8. How does your record compare? ____________________
9. What act of service will you perform this week? ____________________

CHALLENGE ACTIVITY: Skim through the book of Jonah and write down your impressions of the service given by this prophet.

LESSON 32

Hospitality

1. What is the best hospitality you've experienced? __________
   What is the worst? __________
2. What made these experiences good or bad? __________
3. Complete the chart on hospitality:

Reference	*Host*	*Guests*	*What was offered*
Gen. 18:2–5			
Judg. 13:15			
2 Kings 4:8–10			
Neh. 5:17			
Job 31:32			
Acts 16:14–15			
Acts 16:27–34			
Acts 28:2			

4. What does the Bible say to all of us about hospitality?
   Rom. 12:13 __________ 1 Pet. 4:9 __________
   Heb. 13:2 __________ 3 John 5–8 __________
5. Whose hospitality did Jesus enjoy?

Reference	*Host*	*Other guests*	*What happened*
Matt. 9:9–10			
Mark 14:3			
Luke 7:36–38			
Luke 10:38			
Luke 14:1			
Luke 19:5–7			
Luke 24:29			

6. What hospitality have you offered Jesus? __________
7. What hospitality can teens offer? __________
8. What will you do this week to make someone feel at home? __________

CHALLENGE ACTIVITY: Look for someone at church or school who appears ill-at-ease and uncomfortable—someone on the outside looking in. Offer your friendship and welcome to that person.

LESSON 33

Forgiveness

1. What circumstances make forgiveness easy? ______
2. When is forgiving difficult? ______
3. Why do we need to forgive? (Matt. 18:34–35) ______
4. In these commands to forgive, what additional information do you find?

Matt. 5:44 ______ Rom. 12:20 ______

Mark 11:25 ______ Eph. 4:32 ______

Luke 6:27 ______ Col. 3:13 ______

Luke 17:3–4 ______ 1 Thess. 5:15 ______

5. Study these accounts of forgiveness: (check context for full answer)

Reference	*Who forgave*	*Who forgiven*	*What forgiven*
Gen. 33:4–11	______	______	______
Gen. 45:15	______	______	______
2 Sam. 19:23	______	______	______
1 Kings 1:53	______	______	______
Acts 7:60	______	______	______

6. All these are serious offenses. What is the most serious offense you've suffered? ______
7. Have you forgiven? ______
8. Who needs your forgiveness now? ______
9. Why are you withholding forgiveness? ______
10. What will you do to truly forgive from the heart? ______

CHALLENGE ACTIVITY: Using a concordance (your church or library may have one if you don't), look up references to discover all you can about Jesus' forgiveness of sin.

LESSON 34

Discipling

1. Looking back over the lessons you've completed, what have you gained? ______

______

2. Which of the disciplines are you practicing regularly? ______
3. Which were most difficult to put into practice? ______
4. Which discipline has been most helpful? ______
5. What changes have occurred in your life due to this study? ______

______

6. What is the next step in using what you have learned?

   Matt. 28:19 ______ 2 Tim. 2:2 ______

7. Who discipled whom?

   Deut. 3:28 ______ Luke 6:13 ______

   1 Kings 19:19–21 ______ 2 Tim. 1:1, 2, 13 ______

8. What is God's goal for each new disciple?

   Rom. 8:29 ______ Eph. 4:13 ______

9. What service is essential to pass along what you've learned?

   Mark 3:13–14 ______

   Acts 8:4 ______

   1 Cor. 4:2 ______

   Phil. 3:17 ______

10. Who needs your help to grow in their Christian life? ______
11. What are you willing to do to disciple them? ______

CHALLENGE ACTIVITY: Commit yourself to working with someone through the summer months, sharing the disciplines you've learned. Ask your pastor or other spiritual leader for suggestions on how to disciple. Keep a journal of what happens in both of your lives.